NOT TILL WE ARE LOST

poems

William Wenthe

LOUISIANA STATE
UNIVERSITY PRESS
BATON ROUGE
2004

designer: Andrew Shurtz   *typeface:* Janson Text   *printer and binder:* Thomson-Shore, Inc.

Library of Congress Cataloging-in-Publication Data:
Wenthe, William, 1957–
   Not till we are lost : poems / William Wenthe.
      p. cm.
   ISBN 0-8071-2903-8 (cloth : alk. paper) — ISBN 0-8071-2904-6 (pbk. : alk. paper)
   I. Title.
   PS3573.E565N67 2004
   811'.54—dc21   2003011688

I wish to express my gratitude to the editors of the following journals and anthologies in which poems from this volume have previously appeared, occasionally in different versions or under different titles: *American Literary Review:* "Yerba Canyon"; *Chattahoochee Review:* "Water Dish"; *Chelsea:* "Goldeneye," "Redbud"; *Georgia Review:* "The Daily News," "After Moving to a Place Where I Do Not Know the Names of Plants and Birds"; "W. H. Auden, Leaving Lubbock, Texas, Writes a Sonnet"; *Image:* "Story," "White Settlement"; *Laurel Review:* "Visitations," "Bluebird and Comet"; *Meridian:* "Descansado"; *Orion:* "The Owl on Texas Avenue," "Wildflowers"; *Poetry East:* "American Picture at Lumpkin's," "Nostradamus"; *Press:* "A Photograph of Rilke"; *Southern Review:* "The Music Lesson," "Sentimental Pictures," "Hammering Stones," "The Mysteries"; *Tar River Poetry:* "The Ashes"; *Texas Review:* "Gar," "Trout Fishing in West Texas," "Poet after Stroke."

   "Nostradamus" was reprinted in *Best Texas Writing 1.* "Hammer-ing Stones" was reprinted in *Pushcart Prize XXV: Best of the Small Presses.* "White Settlement" was reprinted in *Texas in Poetry 2.*

   I wish to thank the National Endowment for the Arts, the Texas Commission on the Arts, and Texas Tech University for support in the writing of these poems.

   For their insight and encouragement, I send my gratitude to Robert Cording; to Bruce Beasley, Loren Graham, Suzanne Paola, William Thompson, and Daniel Tobin; to Jeffrey Harrison; to Henry Taylor for his support; and to Jacqueline Kolosov, for all that's beyond words.

Not till we are lost, in other words, not till we have lost the world, do we begin to find ourselves, and realize where we are and the infinite extent of our relations.

— Thoreau, *Walden*, "The Village"

CONTENTS

I　　*. . . for ye are strangers and sojourners with me*
　　　　　—Leviticus 25:23

WATER DISH

It will happen sometimes, in a strange place:
waking surprises us—that rush
of surroundings, startled flush
of creation—for a moment, miracle.

Then, memory. We put on our stories
before our clothes: Oh yes, the motel in Beaumont . . .

Except once. Adam, that first morning,
with a mind only dust
and a divine breath, must have awakened
as no one's woken since—continual
arousal to that warm, enormous light in the air
licking the river, spangled in leaves,
dangling its paws from the lianas.

Even Eve had to open her eyes
to that dubious mirror—his flesh
her history; his future
in her belly. Now,
the world he woke to banished
to story, chapter
and verse, to lurk
on the border of sleep, or, in odd moments,

to pounce: What is that shard of sky
that drops into a ceramic bowl outside my window—
in that instant before
I think it: *blue jay,*
walling myself out with the words?

AFTER MOVING TO A PLACE WHERE I DO NOT KNOW THE NAMES OF PLANTS AND BIRDS

An invisible bird signs his name,
bouncing his song down canyon walls

as one might toss a pebble from the rim.

When I say the word *canyon*, shall I gather
that it holds these breeze-twitched
mustardy flowerets, or the pour
of clouds above rimrock, or shimmering
fox-color grasses on talus?

An evergreen with feathery bark,
the dead one grating against itself—
I have no name
for that, or for the birds flitting
branch to branch, their one note enough
to call each other home.

Never before such variety
of thorns: two-inch spikes on scrub branches
glisten with snagged
sunlight, bristled cactus twisted
like antlers, the ground-plant's cluster of green
rapiers, hooked edges
of flower-husk and leaf—

each pricking an announcement
in my skin to which I have no
reply. And none for the animal that, sensing
my approach, crackles
through underbrush, its disappearance

a kind of mirror,
a terrified name it names me.

SENTIMENTAL PICTURES

They find me now in cheap hotels
Or laundromats, where no one means
To dwell for long. The title, when
There is one, is always "Autumn Scene,"

Opening upon a forest glade
Or rolling field, inviting to the eye;
A world of umbers, ochres, grays,
Basking under an Indian summer sky.

And always, too, a foreground birch
Or wooden fence with open gate—
A trick to show the painter's skill,
And draw you closer to the verge.

I remember them from homes or stores
Visited with my mother when,
Still too young to go to school,
I would go with her everywhere:

Though I was stuck, my eye could wander
Through painted gate and stippled field;
Instead of shoe store, or lady's parlor
Or waiting room, or whatever . . .

Once, I recall, an old-style house,
Hushed voices, an air-conditioned chill,
A woman lying in a polished box
With flowers—absolutely still.

Perhaps they've hung for all these years
In rooms it would take years to enter;
Or maybe they were picked up later,
Dusty in junk shops, church bazaars—

Either way, they still suffice
To fetch my eye. And I suppose
I ought to be a little bit
Ashamed for liking the sort of art

That tells you what you already know—
That clowns are sad, and nature's nice—
And this one's no exception: *Now*,
It says, *is all the time there is.*

Down the vortex of highway falling
from Sangre de Cristo Mountains to open desert, I burn
the straightaways, stealing the most miles
of sun before running smack
into night's deadline. Roadside scrolling blur:
sagebrush and scrub juniper, and the small haphazard
shrines, each in memory of one who
wrecked there: painted boards nailed crosswise,
flowers and the name of the dead fleeting past
too quickly to read—
                              only the mournful word
descansado hanging briefly in my ear.
Ahead in midroad a scrap—
tumbleweed? retread? It takes the shape
of a hawk—I swerve—it *is* a hawk
shivering in the car's windblast.

And now the car half-ditched; the heat and slap
of my sneakers on pavement: I'm flapping
my arms wildly to scare it into flight,
or to slow down the onrush
of a truck looming over the next rise.
Closer: each scallop of feather, the beak's
meathook, its hoof-dark sheen (and such faint
scratches on it)—I didn't think,
when I stopped, of hackles rising
on the back of the head as it twists
to fix me in one gold eye.

What can I do for this hawk?—for what

I am in love with, suddenly and without
argument? Stupidly, boyish, I
nudge a foot towards it—wings flare wide,
beak wields open, pink inner mouth
and pointed tongue. I jump back,
and notice now the other, damaged
eye, swollen and frosted over.

A long, unreasoning groan
of air brakes—but the hawk won't even
flinch, keeps its good eye trained at me . . .

Then windless quiet . . .
                              I strip off
my shirt, drape it over the already
half-blinded thing, who now lets me fold
its wings snug against the body.
When I lift, talons long as finger-bones
pierce the shirt, clutch air. In my hands
the crisp shell of outer feathers, and somewhere
inside them the body's deep weight, more
than I could have imagined:
I am carrying a red-tailed hawk
I repeat to myself like a spell
to keep away the circling thoughts
of something else—
                              my father, blind now in the sheer
overload of his age, whom I can never
heal, and hold back from in fear,
feeling (no talons, no stern eye)
the distance of his otherworldly
life, animal I cannot enter.

Red-flaked rock crumbles under
my feet; I reach as far as the barbs
on a rancher's fence will allow,
untangle my shirt from the hawk, set him
down to die, in a place
less vulgar than the roadway—
even if it means, at dusk,
the hunger of coyotes.

I'm driving home, the sun's
gold eye descending in the rearview; ahead,
rising on the eastern horizon, father night.

HAMMERING STONES

On the gospel channel, bodybuilders:
one rolls up a frying pan, one uncurls
a horseshoe's steel Omega; one lays hands
on a pair of Georgia license plates, rips
them in half. Leather weight-belts, talc,
sweat, glutted veins in bicep, neck;
gnashing teeth, grunts bowel-deep, pecs
that surge and stress the words
on T-shirts: GOD MADE YOU TO WIN.

It's more than just a ten-foot log
one of them cleans and jerks above his head;
nor do they believe the single-mindedness
of the man hammering stones with his forehead
is enough. That something other moves
in the knuckles of the man clobbering nails
into hickory with his fists is concrete
proof: here is Grace made tangible.

In a motel room, the thumb of a man
clicks along the remote, looking
for something to distract him from one
moment to the next. Above the neon lot,
a few stars visible, spiked into the dark;
bats lift *themselves* in jagged wreaths
around the streetlamps. All day, with one foot
and one hand, he moved 2000 pounds of Chevy
across four states. If he can lift tomorrow
his eight pound head from the damp pillow
it will be enough. The sun could do no more.

NOSTRADAMUS

One day our friend told us
sometimes at night a voice
enters her room, and she writes its words
in her diary. She asked if we're familiar
with the name, Nostradamus—for that
is how the voice names itself,
though she had never heard of him.
Because she comes from County Clare,
I thought of Yeats, who grew up as well
in the Irish vales, where I believe
they call it "the gift." So last night,
which was my birthday (and the spring
equinox), we were on our way
to the canyon for a party, but
had only gotten out of the driveway when
I backed the car into the door
of a gold Cadillac, leaving a nice
crater. This is the car
our Irish friend drives, belonging
to the mother of a man dying
of bone cancer, a man our friend
cooks for because she's a specialist
in healing cookery. She makes him
feel better, though death,
who is a more diligent nurse,
seldom lets him hold down his food.
He has only months, maybe weeks,
to live; even so, he was furious
about the damage to the door.
Earlier that evening, she gave me
a birthday gift, a book containing poems
of Rumi, who says that what you lose
will come back in another form—
that the flicker of emotion on
a friend's face in New Jersey is now
a good meal, or the roseate sheen
glinting across the nape of
a mourning dove on a driveway in Texas.

8

And Rumi says we don't know who we are
when we sleep, but I don't think he said
we don't know who we are when we die.
So, I'll say it: We don't know who
we are when we die. Tonight, I'm
trying to figure out what bills
we'll renege on this month in order
to pay the dying man for the door
to his mother's Cadillac. I walk outside,
and the voices of geese murmur beyond
the houses, coming closer, now calling
overhead. Yeats might have seen them
as emblems of the soul, but I can't decide
if I like them better that way, or as geese.
They fly so low; I can even—or is it
almost?—see their pale bellies
vaguely underlit by streetlamps;
above them, the backyard stars.

TROUT FISHING IN WEST TEXAS

It all comes down to wanting what
the land you live on is absolute-
ly unprepared to give. A trout
will need, first of all, water;
then cold water, water that will
not stay still. Like life,
it comes down to
starting in darkness, head-
lights reined tight on road
till sunrise ratchets up behind you,
pans open the tight-lipped horizon
you interrogate ahead, pressing for
hours on the pedal, demanding
a secret, but getting only
signs for towns with "Plain"
and "Dry" and "Level" in their names.
You might drive past Notrees,
or Needmore, leaving behind
any thought of lives held there,
each a peculiar burning
beneath the sun that all the while
's been gaining on you.
And the road imperceptibly
rising, till rangeland admits
a few straggling junipers,
and it all comes down
to admitting that somewhere
in this long burning
of fuel, you'd left West Texas—
the road at last starting to curve.
And when the mountains have turned
from cardboard backdrop to trees
and passageways, and the only
choice is IN, you follow the road
that rises along a falling
stream till at a likely bend
the shoulder eddies out: there you stop,
gaze into an abyss which gives back,

yes, water—the water all
coming down; sun glare ricochets off
clods and shelves of water bright
as arroyos, as tin-metal roofs—
while underneath, invisible, lies
what you're looking for. You
trust they are hungry as well.

YERBA CANYON

Morning fog-lift, the low ridge fretted
with new snow. Heartwood's

glistening flame-tangerine shriek
of a fallen fir tree; we touch
moist shards as we step through the break, one
of many things to be touched—
the pouting lips of white violets, green
trumpets of new shoots.

Now, the melting:
the *rito* swelling and frothed,
frigid with runoff. Where it gnashes
the path, we puzzle out
crossings: a cribwork of leaning
saplings for handholds, a good stick
to prop us across a wet log-
bridge; then laid there
for our return.

Water and light: spectral
prism-purple and scarlet of pendant
drops, sun-shot.

                    —Is this our life, brought
a moment to lustre? Not *like*,
but *part of*; along with the gray
belly of cloud we've almost hiked into—
here snowpack unmelted, mottled
with dirt and the fallen dead
needles (seen from sagebrush levels below,
a perfect whiteness) soon too deep to walk.

So:
tea from a thermos, cheese and an apple,
and the hike down, the same things seen
from the other side. Red-yellow buds
candle the tips of wiry twigs, clusters

of white flowerets on a stalk, reminding us
of heal-all: so many things for which
we've yet to learn the names.

And speaking of the curious name
for this canyon, you mention
a medicinal herb you've heard of
called *yerba santa*, wondering if it grows here.
Who knows? Neither one of us;
though now we step differently—each new leaf,
blossom, shoot, a possibility.

W. H. AUDEN, LEAVING LUBBOCK, TEXAS, WRITES A SONNET

(June, 1939)

To imagine nothingness, yes—
                              but so much of it?
And so—physical? Earth, horizon, sky, unredeemed
by detail: the scroll of hawk flight, or quill of smoke
can do little but ornament this immensity.
Back in England, we'd have to put something here:
dales, cottages, a local pub, a trout stream,
or a good working mine and slag heap, or simply
ruins—if only that church bells might have something
to echo against . . .
                      Out here, one must beseech
a tenth muse: of emptiness, for this vista far out-blanks
the notebook page; it is like death—a border absolute,
and absolutely unpolitical.

                      But should I have come *this* far
from homely habits, habitats? The easy hostelry of Germany,
gray-black cities of the calm façades; there,
it was understood where one could go for underground
diversions—devoured now by Evil
in uniforms. I could believe this space an angel
sent down to wrestle my soul. Like that cowboy
in the bus depot—tall, raw, stuff of epic . . .
                              A year ago I'd have risked it,
approached him on my knees, though a round beating
is all I'd likely limp away with. Now I turn
to you—Chester, dear chum, lolling sleepy-headed
like a young Dionysus, "loggy with vine-must."
I prod your breast pocket for a cigarette—you shudder
as if, at a mere touch, you'd vanish. And long I watch,
draw to my lips the small combustion—ah, love,
our love-brawlings, extensive tongue-mappings—how
they've taken me, again and again, to that contested
borderland of confusion and awe.

Again the heat rises;
sweat bleeds through shirt and trousers, pastes
me to the seat. Since New Orleans, three days
in the belly of this steel whale, this metal hell.

> *A prison midnight: rats and spiders creep.*
> *Between two garlicky quaternions*
> *Apostle Peter's prayed himself to sleep.*

Plains pricked with cactus, spiked with yucca, reeling
to dizzy horizon. Out there, I still can see,
as if they'd followed us from Louisiana woods,
stabbing picks and shovels in the roadside ditch,
a gang of men, chained together, lifting phantasmal
eyes in dark faces to the bus windows—eyes
in which I read a cry . . .

> *(What does one pray for, bound in cuffs and chains,*
> *And first on the hangman's laundry list?*
> *For sleep? A painless death? Deliverance?)*

Strange how, left to my own devices, I could
never have imagined (and I know, for I have tried)
a feeling quite as waste as what surrounds me now,
this unmappable flatness to which I am delivered.
I've studied the names on maps—*Las Cruces,*
Santa Fe—sounded their landscapes on my tongue.
Spanish—such fond intentions—me! a tourist
visiting a civil war. Now I would not be in love
with any ideal at all. Ahead, I can only see
how the road, this straight and narrow, bisects horizon
like crosshairs on a gunsight; the gun I held in Spain—held,
and aimed, but never fired . . .
                              and telegraph poles repeating,
repeating, their vacant cross-trees. One can barely hope
to remember where we're headed—something about the grave
of Lawrence, my favorite pagan, lying in the thin
air of lofty mountains.

What mountains?
Is this space so tremendous it can hide the Alps?

> *He dreams an angel takes him by the wrist*
> *—suddenly unshackled—and a shining face*
> *Says, "Get your robe on, I've no time to waste."*

Now, this feeling (war fully stricken
from my itinerary) of defeat, no, surrender—marvelous
as this man at my side—surrender to the word
I embrace like shackles, though I say it to no one but
myself . . .

> *A dreamy light enlarges the room. A space*
> *Where the door, bolted, barred, had hung. They walk*
> *Past hallway guards still snoring in their place.*

Maps only lead us to a place; once there, we must
devise our lives.
                And always something more,
eluding the cartographer's art—even in this barrenness
something that surprises, beyond wit, beyond the traveler's
most earnest planning, beyond even the shudder
of rhyme . . .
                the infinite, enduring
variable—a scent breaks through bus windows,
breathing of grass, sweet earth. Eyes,
blinking at horizon's wire, hurt . . .

> *Outside the walls, he does a double-take:*
> *The angel's gone—and Peter's wide awake.*

II   *And it came to pass, as they journeyed from the East, that they found a plain in the land of Shinar; and they dwelt there.*
—Genesis 11:2

WHITE SETTLEMENT

Early September, the weather temperate again;
the autumnal, suburban routines in place:
children with bright backpacks walking to school,

and a little later, the distant noise of drums
from the college band, at practice. Me at my desk,
viewing a snapshot that came from a friend

in yesterday's mail: a group of us, some years ago
in Virginia, standing squint-eyed under strain
of sunlight. On the back she'd scribbled:

> *Found this photo while un-*
> *packing, made copies for all.*
> *I'm sorry, but shots of the*
> *cemetery were badly under-*
> *exposed—it was just too dark*
> *in there.*

"There" was a tangle of blackberry, sweet gum
and sassafras; further in, a space freeing up
beneath limbs of antebellum beech:

in leaf-shadow and tobacco-dark loam, slabs
of knee-high stones upcropped like bad teeth,
like carcass ribs. We had to kneel down

to read the letters and numbers carved there.
I recall the scent of wet stones, the gloss
of moss hiding names and dates we fingered

into legibility. No crosses, no promises—
the Masters' wordy faith too much, perhaps, for hands
that had scratched with nail or knifeblade:

willam hasson
bon 1819
did 1855

The letters were a mix of script and print,
some backward, some skewed, some missing altogether.
Still we sensed behind them something more,

a human presence mingled with the dead
leaves, tangled in creepers, echoed in sculpted
silence of afternoon birdsong lull.

In the snapshot, we've just emerged
from the thicket, its swarm of shadows
still behind our backs, but already forced

to the flatness of paper, like this writing
I attempt in order to make sense of what,
for an hour, I could see, and touch, and breathe.

When I look up from the page, my eyes enclose
this rented backyard, its privacy-fenced corners
sliced into a land I've not yet come to

understand. In dry washes breaking away
to the canyon outside of town, sharper eyes,
I'm told, can find the telltale edges

of arrowheads, or, far older, the chipped tools
of earliest hunters. But I've only read
the drive-by history engraved on a steel

plaque in a park named for the Cavalry Colonel
who destroyed the last villages of Comanche, Kiowa,
Southern Cheyenne—its prose, so carefully

subordinated, leading to a final justification:
thereby opening Western Texas to White settlement.
If soil is another history, then the hard

pavements of parking lots unfurled
at the business-edge of town, the clean slates
of lawns are a cultivated emptiness,

an amnesia . . . All morning,
the nagging brass of the college band rehearsal
has risen from their practice lot, marched

across the path I'd hoped to remember,
negotiating through bramble of my own sentences,
back to a place where illiterate stones

allowed me a glimpse of what always lies
unsaid, unsettling, unspeakable, beneath
our feet. Starting and stopping,

the band's been playing strains
of the national anthem, over and over,
trying to get the ending just right.

THE MUSIC LESSON

A TV clip from the fifties:
Leonard Bernstein twitching his shoulders
through a peppery rendition of William Tell Overture,
then telling his audience of children,
"I know you think this is about cowboys and Indians,
and I'm so sorry to disappoint you,
but it's not; it's about notes."

That was the tough-love lesson for the week:
the world of art is rigorous, ideal;
we keep our clutter out of it. But today,
a man rang our doorbell, pitching a ploy
along the lines of Bernstein's cagey
joke on the kids: little signs that say,

> *This house protected*
> *by silent alarm*
> *monitored 24 hours.*

He was trying to cash in on a rash
of break-ins in our neighborhood. "You see,"
he smiled, "with this you won't need an alarm—
the only thing better is a big, loud dog!"
He was a nice guy and, being a good
salesman, was a bit of a performer,
keeping us enthralled like kids.

As his slick spiel flowed, slowly his words
oozed toward the kids of the other color,
the other language, implying that they
were the guilty ones. And he expected us
to know that. So, I note, we *are*
talking about cowboys and Indians, after all.
And each sign he sells is connected to
an intricate, subtle, and most silent alarm.

And Bernstein? Even he—a great, a demanding artist—
had tried, hard, to lever what power he had
against bombs falling in crescendos

on Cambodia. And in our neighborhood,
my wife and I, because he was a nice guy,
buy a couple of signs, and stick them
in a kitchen drawer, where they sleep,
cluttered with other oddments of our house.

AMERICAN PICTURE AT LUMPKIN'S

I don't so much see it as recognize it:
this offset print, framed above the to-go counter
of Lumpkin's Restaurant where I stop each day
on my way to work. It is a sunny morning
in a world faded toward the uniform
gray-blue of prints left too long
in real sun. The artist would have us believe
the elements of this scene could all happen together
in one space: that this split-level suburban home
and crewcut lawn could border flawlessly
a busy barnyard with its classic red barn;
that church steeples and smokestacks could so
amicably define the distant townscape, contained
so nicely on the horizon.

In the center of it all, a boy whirls up
on his rearing pony. I know him well.
His hair is combed and shellacked till it shines
like a helmet; he is wearing blue jeans,
but they are called dungarees, and they have cuffs.
This much of his life I remember. He's just off to,
or back from, a magnificent adventure
that I can't remember, because he's the one who,
somewhere along the line, took my place forever,
and climbed into this picture, where,
for the moment, he grandstands.

And what a moment it is: his dog scampers
under the horse legs, a goose bursts out of the way;
his sister in her apron feeds the little chicks,
while his mother in her apron, and the hen, watch over.
Dad waves from the conveyor belt tumbling bales
of hay to the brimming hayloft, where Eb is stacking them
for the cattle, now lined up in the barn, pumping milk
into the amazing new machines. Zeke cuts the lawn by the house
where the crisp-finned Chrysler cozies up to the motorboat,
and an airplane zooms overhead, off to its own
adventure. A streamlined diesel rounds the curve,

connecting town to country in a blast of steel and speed.
And this moment (I noticed one day from the copyright
stamped on the corner) takes place in 1957.
The year that I was born.

The artist, too, seems to have remembered
the way a boy might gather all of his toys
together, and arrange them in one tableau, at once
reassuring and surreal. For there's just too much
happening in this picture: I didn't mention the family
of pigs smiling in the foreground, or the cat and her file
of kittens, who scowls like a gargoyle at the turkey
I didn't mention either, along with the bluster
of pigeons around the barn-roof coop, or the TV antenna
(they called it an aerial) bristling from the house.
The only thing left out is the noise—imagine
the racket—pigs squealing, dog barking, cows mooing,
ducks—did I mention the ducks?—quacking . . . lawnmower,
conveyor belt, milking machine, airplane, locomotive—
no wonder the horse is rearing! I'm wishing now
that I could wait another second, just to see
if that horse will topple him at last—a good clocking
with a horse hoof ought to tell him:

Get on with your life,
kid. Haven't you had it too good
for too long? This American dream painted here
is like any dream—there are elements
off in a corner, shadows with no faces: important
just because they're hid. A couple of years, and your dad
will discover this land's more valuable
as a shopping mall. You'll move to that town
with something between your legs more terror
and joy than any pony. Go there, and some day
you'll walk into a diner with a name like Lumpkin's;
you'll pass me there, as I head out to the car,
place my coffee precariously on the dash,
then drive to work, trying to make sure it won't spill.

Strange, Rilke, to find you waiting *here:*
this dumpy railway station, which can't afford
a platform roof, whose tracks serve double-duty
for a chain of freight cars looming at your back.
Doubtful that conductor, peering between gas lamp
and telephone pole, would recognize the famous
poet, or the elegant woman at your side;
still he looks on, sensing, it seems, your discomfort,
embarrassment even, to be the subject of a mere
snapshot. Your face—fit for portraits in oil—
appears only as a blur, as if refusing
to resolve itself into this moment
a new-fangled technology attempts to record.

Judging by the scratches, this photo was no cherished
souvenir, but one long neglected in a drawer.
And yet I'm writing now from memory—
this image haunting me like your poem's image
of a bat's flight cracking the porcelain of night sky;
or your impossible wish, recorded elsewhere:
to play a phonograph needle upon
the wave-like sutures of the skull, and sound
the primal origins of lyric cry.

Your posture—leaning forward, shoulders
hunched, as if cringing from those hopper cars,
that thoroughly un-angelic tank car—
tells that you hate this place—you
who preferred a friend's chauffeured automobile,
whose Muse checked into first-class
hotels, who'd rather view the smokestacks
of Elberfeld from the industrialist's
mansion where you stayed, pampered guest
too good for mere wage work, your poetry
too important. Thus your courtship of the rich—
countesses whose family names resisted
time, castles that walled off the encroaching
century. Sheltered there, you sang

to selfishness disguised as solitude—
but I can't say that I hold you to blame:
for if poetry were to save anyone,
wouldn't it have to begin with you?
You know it won't save many—it wouldn't save
the beautiful woman clinging to your arm,
this rising young actress who, it is recorded,
thirty years later in Auschwitz perished.

THE OWL ON TEXAS AVENUE

Six empty lanes wide, Texas Avenue measures
in cobbles glinting of a July noon, departures:

descendants of whores and buffalo hunters,
the downtown merchants have followed the herd

to the rolled, rolling asphalts of the malls.
Here, where the aluminum trim peels away

from the awning of the old Whatever store, a shade
for walkers back when walkers grazed here

(display windows dusty-black as blackboards now),
sits surely one of the odder sights in town:

an owl, of plastic molded; a generic,
an art director's idea of, owl; vaguely "Great Horned"—

sporting the ear-tufts but no white throat—
but otherwise painted to ape the real

owl, down to the toes, like feathery starfish
stranded up there on a plastic rock.

It was taken from its original home
in a gardening store, and introduced here

for purpose of frightening pigeons away—
those same pigeons milling about its feet.

Bum-pigeons, shabby, down-at-heels,
blended by default with their surroundings:

little they remember how to be prey. Likewise
disinherited from the *genuine* (from the root

to beget), this mock-owl, this mule, this bastard owl
knows nothing of owl; only disingenuousness persists

in calling it "owl," or in saying that it gazes
straight into the cocked ear of a satellite dish

placed before the thing like the gramophone
before the Victor Dog, as if it held

some sort of information, some remembered voice.

First furl of light, a planet or two
still looms in backlit sky.
Whatever it was that scuttled
my sleep, brought me to the window,
is gone; only the far, discernible shriek
of a rooster that someone, oddly
enough, keeps in the city, slips
through the walnut and myrtle.
A small groin ache is a mark
of how our bodies scored the night, hurtling
toward each other—toward something far other,
like two gods trying to hurt
a new world into existence.

Thirty miles away, a trailer hangs on the edge
of cottonfields that pitch toward horizon
flat as a razorblade. Inside, a man
stands sobbing, muttering something
ridiculous, like "Please understand,"
to his two little boys, as he fires
at one, then, apologizing, the other.
He tucks them back under their sheets,
and places the hot barrel in his mouth.

Or maybe that's another day's news,
and today's fate will be the simple notice
of our old neighbor walking with his wife again,
slowed from the stroke that laid her up,
her stiff hand held in crisp salute
to all the gardens and dogs
as she shades her eyes from the sun.

It's all so complicated—all that conspires
to break that man down, hold her together.
We're rolling into it so fast the sun
feels like it really could be a chariot
driven by a kid on a suicidal
joyride, as the newspaper hurled like a missile

whacks at our door.
The planets have blinked
shut, the rooster now mute, and what's left for me
is to wait for a rustling of sheets,
the omen of your waking.

GOLDENEYE

I occupied myself a whole day in watching his movements; on the next I came to a determination as to the position in which I might best represent him; and on the third thought of how I could take away his life with the least pain to him.
—John James Audubon, "Golden Eagle," in *Ornithological Biography*

Still he called them "portraits," these depictions
of corpses, staked out in lifelike postures
on a homemade contraption of sticks and wires;
though often they look quite dead, suspended
on a background painted in by someone else:
tilted sideways, that flying brace
of blue-winged teal could as well be hanging
by their necks in a market stall.
And his five volumes of companion text—
Ornithological Biography—as if it were
as much his own life as those of birds.

•

Late evening, "fatigued and hungry,"
he comes upon a marsh, and avocets,
stalks knee-deep in mud to find the nest.
Next morning, at dawn, he's crouched
in rushes, waiting for them to come forth
and feed: he feeding on the particulars—
how upon landing, one holds its wings aloft
some moments, "balancing its head and neck,"
or raises wings partly, entering deeper water.
Five hours later, midsummer swelter rising,
for an hour he watches them *sleep.*
Wades again to the islet and the nest;
he's crawling now in the mud, all
for the particulars: now three feet away
from the brooding hen, her half-closed eye,
blotches on the eggs, *pear-shaped*, he notes.
Then: "Having . . . obtained all desirable knowledge
of these birds, I shot down five of them."

•

And so from Florida Keys to Labrador, New Orleans
and the Mississippi, the Ohio and upper Missouri,
the continent's great arteries: Taking it in—
shooting game for portraits, and for his meat;
sprinkles gunpowder on roasted flesh for salt.
Waiting for wood ducks, a mosquito
on his hand: he studies the operation,
the flexible needle piercing his skin, pumping
blood, the abdominal sac swelling red,
the lifting of wings, and heavy parting.

•

After two days of trying to suffocate that eagle
with smoking charcoal and sulfur, he punctures
its heart with a sharpened steel rod.
Sleepless, drawing constantly: two days later,
"seized with a spasmodic affection,"
prostrate for two days, attended by physicians.
—"It nearly cost me my life."
In the finished painting, the eagle's talon
pierces the bleeding eye of the hare it hoists
above crags. In a lower corner (and this
omitted from the printed edition), bearded,
buckskinned, a tiny figure of a man—
Audubon himself, it is said—straddles
a log between two cliffs, a shotgun
and a dead eagle slung on his back.
It is slow going: he chops at protruding
branch stubs with his hatchet. At first glance,
he appears to be hacking at the log
itself, the very thing that holds him
above that chasm.

•

Between the real and the representation,
a "necessary murder"—Auden's phrase;
though in another context, and later recanted.
But if not murder in the legal sense,

still something that brings mortality near
to the will—a proximity, a fringing
upon, a falling off or close to it;
a vertigo. I stood in a gallery,
Andres Serrano's photographic studies
of the morgue. Huge cibachromes in black
frames, blown up on the wall—this one
maybe six feet square: filled with breath-
taking swirls of vermilion, constellated
with lozenges of black, the white sequins
of highlights. An abstract formalism,
a colorist's delectation—such that I forget
it is a photo, a close-up of the real, until
I read the title: "Burned to Death."
On one hand, red blood & muscle, skin
charred to carbon; on the other hand,
this photograph, this striking composition;
and in between, suspended, alone,
I stood in a gallery . . .

•

"I cannot help thinking Mr. Audubon has deceived you,"
writes John Keats to his brother in America,
after Audubon had sold him a sunken boat.
Relentless self-promoter, groomer of facts:
his dubious claim to have been the student
of Jacques Louis David, the rumor his mother
might have been Marie Antoinette. But for all
his false representations, the ones that cut him,
snagging back at him like briars, were those
behind his art: to anyone who has observed
"the perfect and beautiful forms of birds,"
he writes, "the representation is not that
of *living* nature!"

                    But *dying* nature? Here,
perhaps, his best chance to get across
that distance: I'm looking at his portrait
of the goldeneye, the duck whose life

he praised in Keatsian diction—"Happy being!";
the surprise of the pair in this painting,
midair, appearing to turn somersaults,
beaks open, exclaiming. He's captured
the male's crisp black-and-white, subdued
grays of the female; the yellow tip of her bill,
the green-black gloss—rarely visible
in the field—glowing on his cheek and brow.
His wing, though, cranks backwards—a flash
of scarlet and yellow rips the wing-shoulder,
a bright epaulette, or ribbon worn for a cause.
The bird's been shot—that flash the gash of meat
and blood—the way his red tongue dips over
his beak—that's not his tongue, it's blood—
compare the female's, still flesh-pink.
One, dark, vermilion drop suspends
from the nostril—that's the giveaway this bird
is dying, that droplet painted in masterly
fashion: shadow to form the bulge of it,
white highlight to show it is live blood—
the clinching, deadly detail.

GAR

In the swollen blister of summer, I'd rise
from bedsheets mud-wet at dawn, descend
through trees' green smoke to the river,
where water flowed orange like lava
toward the sizzling egg of sun in the East.
I'd wade groin deep, casting for bass,
but sometimes these others would surface, gulping
for air, and my spine gave a snake-shudder
at glimpse of the emerging head:
long beak all teeth, the flat immoveable
eye, older than lung and leg and warm blood.
Once in a backwater I found one circling,
a fresh-killed sunfish clamped broadside
in its jaws. I tried to snag it,
jerking treble hooks across the scaly hide
the guidebook likens to armor. Had I cast
a hundred million years I might have come
to know my excitement and my shame—
might have drawn that thing from the dark
water, or sunk with it into the same.

STORY

Last July, mindless
with heat, I saw the neighbor's
cat bound into the path of a car,
then thud backward, its perfect body
a demoralized heap.

Carefully, I gathered him
in a box, and rang the bell.
And I knew by the way she said it—
"We'll have to put him out of his misery"—
she was asking me to do it.

I panicked: How?

All I've known was the feel
of a fist-size rock
& cartilage-crush on the cold mask
head of a fish; the taut
spasm, the stopping.

But that would be too
brutal for her cat;
and the walk down to the pond
would only torture it;
I don't have a gun.

"Do you have a garbage bag?"
I finally asked. "And a rubber band?"
And when I'd rigged it up
"Would you start your car?"
We watched, it seems, with ceremony;

and though I cannot speak for her,
I felt a twinge of,
well, *success* in the efficiency
and humaneness
of my solution.

Then I buried him, replaced
the tools, and washed
my hands at her
sink, and she said,
"Thank you."

As I'm leaving, a flashback:
her shuddering glance, first opening
the door, in that awkward space
before I was recognized,
and I might be anyone.

III   *. . . an offering made by fire, of a sweet savor . . .*
      —Leviticus 1:13

ELEGY IN WAITING

You, stroke-struck, riding that hospital bed—
where are you now?

March winds—first day of spring and my birthday—
by afternoon a gray dust, a sky galvanized,
the old sheet metal of dust
collectors on warehouse roofs, windowless hulks . . .

Not the robin's egg blue,
dove's neck rose and jonquil sky of painted Ascension
in the book of plates I'd taken from the shelf,
because my eyes resist the word-after-word
of reading. Wind-stressed
branches grate on the siding;
not music of Palestrina . . .

Where are you now, *really*, you there riding?

I think of forty years ago: you driving
our old Chevy, when my door sprung open—
and as I fell your right hand, with a will
stronger than gravity, than accident,
pulled me back in.
I still see the rolling pavement lunging toward my head.
Your left hand never lost control of the wheel.
And today your "living will,"
written, executed—

They pulled the tubes bearing fluids.

No story now: only this wait, this
bearing. And the week like a sentence
demands its sequence. I hold the woman
I live with; I show up at class. One evening,
the tickets bought weeks ago to *Die Fliedermaus*,

where it's all a prank staged in formal wear,
with champagne and waltzes.

And all week this tug in the blood—
Who is this who pulls, this pulsing?

I'm under the trees, late at night; the rolling wind's
one blur of sound in my ears, while the cat's charged eyes
discern a thousand motions . . .

Mother, riding the bed of your dying . . .

Hedge-leaves quiver; the rhododendron a chalice
of shadow. And you?

WILDFLOWERS

This is the time of year they return
to the low ridge in Virginia—to me,

nowhere near them now: memories springing up,
unburied, gorgeous in the dirt.

A warm afternoon, walking where the dead
leaves crisp up in sun, the first blue

thrill of hepatica, almost stepped on.
In midwood, patches of daffodil, the last

trace of houses long absorbed
into soil. And further down,

along creekbank, hidden tubers issued
skeins of spring beauties—pink-veined

blossoms hovering in the ribbed sunlight while,
held in the hollow's deep shade

where nights the almost human screams
of mating barred owls reached my house,

trillium unfurled its trinity of pure
white petals, blushing to pink as days

bore on, until finally wizened to brown.
And the whiteness that haunts me most—

simple petals of bloodroot
nestling the gold pollen. Each year,

I let myself pick just one,
pinching the stem apart to prove

its name—the red juices running down
my fingers, staining them all day.

REDBUD

I cut down the cankered
redbud till the chainsaw kicked up
dirt, the trunk a gray scab nailed
to the ground by roots.

Later: red shoots like arrows
fired into it. Fleshy leaves.
I thought of Mishima, haunted
by images of St. Sebastian, always

painted with the drained
and languid expression of after sex,
as if there were joy in that release
of blood, the blossoming wound.

The redbud won't do for me
what Sebastian did for Mishima,
who with a blade carved out
the bouquet of his own bowels.

I'll admit: wounds
transform us in ways beyond
merely dying. A child,
I stared at the picture

of the Sacred Heart: stylized
organ, aflame and pierced
by a crown of thorns, dripping
with convincing blood.

Strong and simple,
universal yet bitingly
personal: why not
worship pain? Like spirit,

it goes beyond the limits
of body: Mishima killed himself
because Japan disdained to remember

the past as he would have it.

Maybe the Christian
punks I've lately noticed
around town know more
than I do: their skin needled

with crucifix tattoos, pierced
with metal studs, they gather
over Bibles in coffee shops.
I will leave them

their symbols; and the redbud
is only a diseased organism
obeying the simple law
of earth, water, and sun;

though every morning I stare
at those red shoots, those leaves,
as if I, too, refuse
to let go of the tree that it was—

that flame-flourish at Easter.

VISITATIONS

The Virgin Mary's on the Evening News
again. From time to time her face
is found in some unlikely spot
in Texas: the raveled bark-gnarl
of a cottonwood in Brownsville, or cracks
on a plaster wall in Lubbock. The video clip
shows her contours clear enough,
as though it's not so much a matter
of belief, as of interpretation:
What's she *doing* in that tree, that wall?

Perhaps she tells us to remember
what we were taught by fairy tales
and miracles: that mystery hinges on
the ordinary—once, she appeared in cheese mold,
a fortunate fall of lightning
that knocked refrigerators out for days.
Or it may be she's merely tired
of pedestals, golden crowns and votive
candles, and wants to be known as one
who once liked simple things—stitching a cloth,
fetching a jug, tossing crumbs in the alley—
before God's bird roosted in her womb.

She was, according to the gospel, "troubled,"
which makes me wonder if she's not
choosing this at all—perhaps she's drawn
down here in servitude, to plaster and cheese
and bark of cottonwood, to all
the people needing her in any form: "Handmaid
of the Lord," perhaps she's never had a form
quite her own—all these appearances
the monstrous shapes of someone else's will.

This time, it's the outline of road dust
on the hood of an '81 Camaro in
the border town of Elsa. As usual,

the church itself takes no position;
the TV station sends its youngest reporter
to play up the quaintness angle. Among the gathered
faithful, are those who mumble prayers at her,
others who would rather listen
to the inscrutable silence of dust.

Yesterday a bluebird, all tail-flash
and wing-blur, smacked
the porch windows, flung himself against
his own reflection. Mad
with March hormones, he was drawn in
and beaten back by that spectacular
image of his compulsions. Behind
the window's one-way mirror, I
observed him closely, till he slumped ex-
hausted on the sill where—as if surprised
to remember it's all about mating—he sang!

At night I walked into the shadow
behind the barn, looking for the light
of a comet the weatherman had promised
the naked eye could see, for a few nights
of its aeon-long orbit. I saw nothing
but stars; then, after the length of a smoke,
a blur, like a firefly in mist. Binoculars revealed
a larger blur, which trembled with the trembling
of my hands. How was I to know
that is what a comet looks like?

Later my father, who's lost almost all
his eyesight, wanted me to show him
the comet. I let slide the obvious
question; only led him to the shadow
of the barn, considering how I might
describe for him what he wouldn't see.
Instead, he pointed to the glow my eyes
had barely discerned, and said "That must be it."
And it was: brighter now, a wisp of tail
feathering out behind.

And then he asked me what I know
of planets, pointing to the one I took
to be Jupiter, the rusty spark I guessed
was Mars—having no idea

if I was right, or no idea at all
what he actually saw: that hand aimed
toward gleams in the universe the same
hand that gropes the kitchen table
for a fork, a coffee cup—the same hand
I'd seen that morning holding
my mother's hand as she wept, vexed
with her slow orbiting back from a stroke.

I'd come a long way
to help them out; thinking, too,
to briefly leave the push and pull
of my own marriage, which seldom reveals itself
as what we thought we'd find there.
But now I'm only baffled at my parents'
decline: barely a body between them
whole enough to keep a house, and still
they persist, keeping to their rounds
of chores, habitual as birds . . .

Morning I'm at the window again,
waiting for the bluebird, my beating mind
still thinking of the force that keeps them
moving, which must be something
like the shadow of the barn that uncovered
my father's sightedness for stars.
Whatever it is, I like to think
is something beyond the comet's merely
gravitational affair with the sun, the bluebird's
instinctual urge—though I have to admit,
because I partly admire him,
I'm drawn back to that maddening
blue flare, the brilliant
surrender giving way to song.

POET AFTER STROKE

A writers' conference: I'm talking, talking,
With students as teacher, teachers as student.
Workshop finished, I'm looking for the phone when
      Somebody stops me—

Hand on my elbow, the other extended
Toward an old man who is heaped on a sofa,
Propped by a cane. And with the introduction
      I'm almost broken,

Hearing his name: I'm victim of a mugging;
Now held like a hurt robin; style and judgement
Have written me a letter—which is to say
      I've read his poems.

He holds forth a crimped hand; somehow I manage
A way to hold it. He is one side granite,
One side rockslide. Slowly, he mouths, *Fifteen years*
      Ago I was silent.

It was hard—I was very . . . The half of him
That can, is smiling: *Can't find—the word.* We tell him
It's alright, filling the gap with assurances,
      Trite phrases, triter

For being true. More than alright: his silence
Reveals what's at stake. Then it comes: *Ornery!*
Boy on a ropeswing, he plops on the word as
      If it were water—

Each year—my speech is better—I am happy.
He turns to me—eyes which nothing's diminished,
Surely no metaphor of my own making—
      You? Are you happy?

THE RED SOFA

Today is your birthday, two weeks after
your death day. And April too full of itself
to notice. New grass stalks, not yet under
the first cutting, toss their manes of small seed.
Sun glints off the countless filaments, which cross
each other, glint upon shadow, shadow
upon glint, wind-multiplied. Bees
probe the myrtle's pale-green blossoms
no bigger than a bee's head.

If I were to misread it all, say it were a feeling—
this moment of a day so insistent upon recurrence—
it might be taken for joy.

Closer, the straw weave of last summer's grass
beneath the flickering growth; on my sill, crossed
arms of the dead wasp, the pale-green house spider.
Even the elm is half bone, bare limbs
among the leaves: the habit that trees keep
of living and dying at once. And the sun, leaving,
burns them with a Byzantine gold, a gold leafing.

I know if I were to play music, those movements
built on promises fulfilled
in time, it would flay me with grieving.

The trees' old sermon: that there is no difference.
But what I kissed when I kissed the cold forehead
was not you: skin of stone, a smooth-grained
enamel on the bone. Your body that delivered me
—ferry I rode to this living—was a thing to be loved
no longer: some parcel left behind on the pier,
waiting only for disposal by fire.

Now mother, you are the difference. To summon you,
I summon the boy on the red sofa, evenings
when he sat with you, and learned to read.

The cone of light from the red-shaded endlamp;
your voice curled about my own, sounding
the letters—how their curious limbs began
to move, limbs and sounds emerged as words
the way that, following a pointing finger,
I've seen reeds quiver, and the marsh become a bird;
and word after duckling word the tale unspun
across the red sofa, in the coneflower glow
of your arms. And so the beginning of
reading, when I learned of beginnings,
and so of endings. And here began the grieving.

So writing's rooted in losing, that once-trendy lesson.
But to keep writing, when the you I'm writing to
is nowhere I can tell—such writing is something
other—gesture or motive—a keeping, a prayer.

Dawn now, or almost. No birdsong, but the first
printing of black limbs on sky, a Byzantine blue.
A dream pushed me awake—the one
I'd been waiting for, as if it were
an appointment. In the dream, we're driving
in the '55 Chevy—remember?—only I'm
at the wheel, you on the bench seat beside me.
The wide windshield takes in a narrow road
we're traveling somewhere curves will not disclose:
only sunlight, and the countless waving hands
of broad-leafed maples. We were talking—so much
to say—and I don't remember a single word.

The assembly of day. Again, again. And nothing
the same. But who are you and who am I
is the same question. Of answers, the best I have
is what I give when I give thanks.

THE ASHES

After his funeral, we stirred
        Back to his apartment
To parcel out our father's things.
        Opening up a cabinet,
My brother said, "Oh—
        Sorry Mom, pardon me."

And there she was—a plastic
        Cylinder of ashes,
Stored there with an assortment
        Of cards, words that distant
Friends had sent to him.

        Among us, we passed her
Around, our eyes getting wet,
        —But hadn't they been that way
All morning? It was, mostly,
        A kind of curiosity,
An almost idle,
        "Well how about that?"

Of course it wasn't *her*. She,
        In the words of the priest,
Would be greeting my father,
        Robing him in a scintillant
Garment of soul—one of the ways
        We talk to ourselves
About how we live in bodies

        And wear them out.
Fittingly, the cylinder
        Read, "Warning:
Temporary Container"
        —Referring to her ashes,
Or the thing that held them?
        Our hands were ashes,

That held her. And at that moment,
      In another part of town,
My father's body,
      That hurt him so much
His last weeks, trying
      To leave it, was a rising
Conflagration, a pile of fire
      And quiet sifting.

THE MYSTERIES

What you look hard at seems to look hard at you.
— Gerard Manley Hopkins

I.

My reflection hangs on nothingness, a faded
ghost inside the window-glass, or rather
outside, hovering twenty stories over
Chicago, among snowflakes aglow with the city's
ambient light. The boundless snowflakes swirl,
like schooled fish turning on a hidden axis
inscrutable as instinct, the curved helix
(which now they resemble) of DNA, or the whorl
of fingerprints . . . though every single one
is a fingerprint. At times they look quite lost,
halting before the glass like travelers
befuddled in a hall of hotel doors—
like me, earlier tonight, having just
arrived in this cold, unfamiliar town.

II.

Arrived? In this cold, unfamiliar town
the word sounds jarringly inadequate.
Arrival's what Odysseus did in Ithaca;
but here, this single room just tells me how
alone I am, my marriage newly failed.
But if I think of family history,
I'm led right back to here—one Friedrich Wenthe,
Bavarian immigrant carrying hod.
He had a son named Herman, a printer's devil
who worked his way to owner of the firm,
and hoped his sons would carry on the name;
but the oldest son became a priest, the second
a victim of an auto wreck, and so it fell
to the son who'd someday be my father, Raymund.

III.

But the son who'd someday be my father
found one of the Baptist managers,
the year that Al Smith ran for president,
printing off some anti-Catholic verse
and punched him out, there on the shop floor.
In '37 he married Betty Neil—
"prettiest girl in Chicago"—or so he swore
to me, after sixty years and married still.
They are my parents, a word that comes to me
fraught with stories happening before
my birth, a past that is and isn't mine—
a past of words I trace from memory
like verbal photographs of ancestors
in spectral whites and faded sepia tones.

IV.

Spectral in white and faded sepia tones
of snow and copper streetlamp glow, the city
is just a faint impression of itself, sketchy
but real as stories my parents handed down.
Spectral and real, I turn to them for rest;
though not such words as stitched my parents' faith
in their religion, nursed them through the birth
of their nine children, of which I was the last.
And even with my birth, a shroud of words
recalled: a snowy night like this, it seems
my neck had gotten tangled in the cord;
placed in an incubator, there I spent
my first few days, another "brave infant"
unwilling, I sometimes think, to leave the womb.

V.

Unwilling to leave the womb: I sometimes think
that's why I gravitate to window seats

like this one, overlooking city streets
but sheltered behind glass—my own fish tank.
Cozy in this amniotic warmth,
I count the bridges—six—across the river;
each car, bus, truck, and cab a shuttle weaving
and unweaving the city's endless cloth.
Like Penelope's, this weaving seems to lead us
nowhere; and yet she knew that it had something
to do with a long-awaited coming
home. And so I wonder what to make of
my arrival in this town: which would it be—
a joyful, sorrowful, or glorious mystery?

VI.

The Joyful, Sorrowful, and Glorious Mysteries
are what my family used to murmur through
in Lent, when, gathered in the living room
we prayed the movements of the rosary.
There's Ray and Betty, most of the nine kids
(an older one or two away at college)
counting, bead by bead, along the stages
of *Our Father*s, *Hail Mary*s, *Glory Be*s.
On couch and chairs, we made a kind of circle,
each of us a bead, each bead a voice,
the voices linked in rhythmic unison
worshiping the single life of Christ
until, arriving at the last *Amen*,
we scattered back to individuals.

VII.

Now, scattered to our individual
adulthoods, a pin placed on the map for each
of us would look like broken rosary beads,
or unconnected dots—a child's puzzle
I'm staring at the way, all night, I've watched
the river's frozen skin, sliced by fireboats

into jigsaw pieces, heal, like platelets
in the bloodstream annealing what's been scratched.
And I'm the child who, pen in hand, would draw
those dots together again, heal the wound
of separateness carved into my life—
a wider wound now, separated from my wife.
But are these searched-out words enough—as though
by the very act of searching, it were found?

VIII.

By the very act of searching, it is found—
or so Augustine said, of seeking God,
since God's the source of seeking, the very ground
of need, by which all need's fulfilled.
Human love, he said, is like a travesty
of God's (although I hope he's wrong on this),
directed as it is toward human frailty;
but looking back on ours, I must confess
I thought that loving her made all the wrong
turns right—an arrival, yes—a destiny.
—Until our separate pulses proved too strong;
and so the Joyful leads to Sorrowful Mystery:
which means the question now before me is,
how can the Sorrowful lead to Glorious?

IX.

Or *can* the Sorrowful lead to Glorious?
If you're no believer, it's not a given;
and Chicago seems so far from heaven.
Transcendence is one thing that can't be grasped
alone—one enters it like marriage, a loss
of singleness; but that's a faith I've seen,
like the river's freshened sheet of ice, turn
cold and separate. But maybe there are ghosts
to help me—the trochaic pulse of German
fathers: Friedrich, Herman, Raymund. If not

in spirit, they are here in body: mine—
those rosaries of DNA, determined
and determining, reaching backward but
now arrived, in me, at the end of their line.

x.

When I arrive at the end of a line,
another kind of mystery emerges—
the rhythmic tug, the overlapping urges
of verse traversing back and forth in time:
the way syllabic repetitions rhyme
what's gone with what is now, and prophesy
a future seeded in the present. A sorcery
of sorts, for time moves through the poem
as the poem moves through time. Augustine knew:
the whole psalm happens in the syllable.
In the same way, he said, a life moves through
the heartbeat, a family through individuals;
something pulsing, untranslatable,
that reaches from the single to the whole.

xi.

Reaching from the single to the whole,
my starting point the mystery of loneliness;
if not exactly glorious, nonetheless
familiar—as much my life as Father's tale
of Herman, *his* father, smoking a cigar
while swimming the breaststroke in Crystal Lake.
See: that woven water will also cloak
myself someday, and touches on me here,
companions me as now I look across
the window's doubled pane, into a blizzard
of arrival: where silent crystals, syllables
of settled whiteness taking in the city,
fall and rise in moving patterns, pierce
my reflection hung in nothingness—or cradled.

IN MEMORY OF:

Elizabeth Wenthe 1915–2000
Raymund Wenthe 1910–2000